Facsimile Edition

Harry N. Abrams, Inc., Publishers

A B C Dogs

by

CLARA TICE

ISBN 0-8109-1958-3

This is a facsimile edition of ABC Dogs, first published in 1940
by Wilfred Funk, Inc. The original edition of ABC Dogs was produced
from colored etchings by Clara Tice and hand-lettering
by George L. Carlson, Ludlow Black Type, New York

Published in 1995 by Harry N. Abrams, Incorporated, New York
A Times Mirror Company

Printed and bound in Japan

To my two greatest dogs—

Varna O'Valley Farm
(My Wolfhound)

Jicky
(My Sealyham)

WHO WAS CLARA TICE?

by Marie T. Keller

Clara Tice with Varna, her Russian Wolfhound, and Shezi, her Pekingese. Photograph by Nickolas Muray, 1924

When ABC Dogs was first published, in 1940, critics hailed the publication as "charming," with "all the lively fantasy for which the artist has long been noted." Unfortunately, today the life and work of this talented artist/illustrator are all but forgotten, and Clara Tice—a woman once hailed as the "Queen of Greenwich Village," whose friends included Marcel Duchamp, Edna St. Vincent Millay, Frank Crowninshield, and many other noted early twentieth-century art and literary figures—remains an unknown but important contributor to the history of her time.

Clara Tice was born in Elmira, New York, in 1888, and around the turn of the century came to New York City with her family. She enrolled at Hunter College, but ended her studies there when she decided to pursue a career in art, taking classes with the renowned painter and teacher Robert Henri. With Henri, John Sloan, and others, she figured prominently in the organization of what was to be one of the pivotal art exhibitions of the century: the First Independents Exhibition in 1910. Tice participated in planning the exhibition and, although far from wealthy, even supplied financial assistance to help secure the exhibition hall. She showed twenty-one paintings and was one of only two artists who sold work the opening night.

Tice became famous for her sketches of lithe young female nudes, and for the ease with which she conveyed a sense of action in her work. In March 1915, she skyrocketed to public attention when Anthony Comstock, the leader of the Society for the Suppression of Vice, tried to confiscate her drawings—which friends had informally pinned to the walls of Polly's Restaurant in Greenwich Village. The subsequent publicity brought Tice to the attention of Guido Bruno, the legendary bohemian entrepreneur and proprietor of Bruno's Garret (a popular second-floor bistro on Washington Square), who hosted her first one-person exhibition in May of 1915—a show that included over two hundred fifty drawings and paintings. She soon became a featured artist in many of Bruno's ephemeral magazine-like *Chap Books* and contributed illustrations to a variety of New York newspapers, including the *Times*, *World*, *Globe*, *Evening Mail*, *Sun*, and *Tribune*, along with a number of avant-garde literary ventures such as *Rogue*.

With her gamin-like demeanor (she was only five feet tall and never weighed more than a hundred pounds) and penchant for unusual garb, Tice personified the image of the Greenwich Village artist. Notorious for her bobbed hair (she proudly claimed to have sheared her locks long before Irene Castle), she was more often than not seen in the company of her beloved Russian Wolfhound, Varna—one of the dogs to whom ABC Dogs is dedicated and probably one of the first Russian Wolfhounds bred in the United States. The graceful contours of this dog were perfectly suited to Tice's elegant linear style.

In June of 1915, Tice's caricature of the sculptor and art patron Gertrude Vanderbilt Whitney marked her first contribution to *Vanity Fair*, where Frank Crowninshield had recently assumed the position of editor in chief. Under his leadership, this magazine had become a showcase for the most advanced art and literature then being produced in New York. Crowninshield, who wrote the introduction to ABC Dogs, was to become Tice's ardent admirer and lifelong friend. He published her black and white sketches in *Vanity Fair* on a regular basis, and from 1915 through 1921, she portrayed a variety of subjects for the magazine. With her skill at depicting movement, she was often assigned to cover the ballet, as well as prize fights and other sporting events at Madison Square Garden. Her caricatures displayed a knack for capturing the fopperies and pretenses of society and attracted yet another advocate: the art critic, writer, and caricaturist Carlo de Fornaro. Fornaro was captivated by her Gallic qualities, insisted that she was a direct descendant of Voltaire (he even likened their profiles), and compared her style to that of the French painter Marie Laurencin.

Tice also illustrated many special and limited edition books, several commissioned by the somewhat risqué Pierre Louÿs Society. Illustration, however, was but one facet of her diverse artistic career. She participated in many group exhibitions and, during her lifetime, mounted at least seven one-person shows of her paintings, drawings, and prints. She created the "Peacock" curtain for the short-lived but notorious Thimble Theater of Charles Edison, son of the famous inventor, painted a mural of Deauville beach scenes for the walls of the cabaret Rendez Vous, and designed display windows for Saks Fifth Avenue.

With other Greenwich Village artists and writers, she helped to organize many of the fancy-dress balls popular at the time, and often designed the posters and invitations. The costumes she created for these events were legendary, perhaps none more so than her famous "steam radiator costume," which, with her arms and neck painted silver, she wore to the Greenwich Village Silver Ball in December of 1916 and to the Independents Ball of 1917.

Along with these many professional accomplishments, Clara Tice was known for her passionate love of animals, most particularly dogs. She owned at least a dozen different dogs over the course of her life and desired to possess one of every breed. Tice once confided to an interviewer that she felt differently about dogs than did most other people; "animals enjoy living," she said. They "are more fun than people." The sensitively drawn, delicately colored illustrations in ABC Dogs, and its whimsical but authoritative text, eloquently prove her point.

After living for many years in Connecticut, Tice returned to New York, where she wrote ABC Dogs. There she spent her last years drawing and painting in a tiny apartment in Forest Hills, where she tended to sick and injured animals. She died at the age of eighty-four in 1973.

A BIT ABOUT MISS TICE

It is only the most attractive and charming people who will feel the full charm of this album. Its vogue amongst those who are selfish and socially undesirable — the kind of monsters who dislike dogs, for example — is likely to be circumscribed.

The dogs which Clara Tice has revealed to us are of a quite superior order. They are so exceptional, in fact, that the book might be called a Social Register of dogs. Not a Who's Zoo of Dogs — for that would include too vast and too motley a company for even so warm-hearted a lady as Miss Tice — but a really restricted list of the smart and exclusive dogs we so often meet in the great arena of society.

But, in Clara Tice, we find a lady who has not only met with the critical approval of every manner of dog, but has, as an artist (and in a great variety of books, etchings, murals, posters and paintings) glorified and ennobled them as well. In all her drawings and canvasses, this young artist has discovered a great truth; namely, that any work of art which is conceived with the sole idea of pleasing a patron, has a way of dying still-born; whereas, if it were only designed to delight the creator herself, it has already gone a considerable way toward immortality.

We can sense, in this album, that Miss Tice's canine friendships have been of the happiest possible nature; sense, too, that her sympathy for dogs has been all-embracing; that it has included the pedigreed and the mongrels, the dotards and the puppies, the perennially frisky, and those that are dying of a broken heart.

Frank Crowninshield

A IS FOR AFGHAN

the dressy dog, who wears a topknot on his head. He seems to be wearing a coat and pants too, because of the way the hair grows on his legs. He has a strange loose walk, something like a monkey, and he is tall and strong and can travel for long distances over uneven ground. He is the oldest dog in the world. Thousands of years ago the Egyptians knew the Afghan Hound, but they called him the Cynocephalus, which is quite a mouthful.

B IS FOR BULLDOG

who would never win a beauty contest. He has powerful jaws and short bow-legs, and a shambling walk that reminds you of a sailor. He is the mascot of Yale University, and for hundreds of years he has been the National Dog of England. He doesn't bark, and in spite of his fierce looks he is good natured, playful and a fine faithful friend.

C IS FOR COCKER SPANIEL

whose soft eyes and silky ears make friends for him wherever he goes. He keeps his friends too, because he is obedient, playful and faithful. Once he lived in Spain and was sent to an English king as a gift. Soon he became a favorite pet, not only in the royal household but among other people as well. Because he came from Spain the English called him "Spaniel" and he was so fond of hunting woodcocks that they gave him "Cocker" as a first name.

D IS FOR DALMATIAN

but he moved from Dalmatia so long ago that we probably know him better as the Coach Dog. He used to be a pointer, and he is also particularly fond of horses. In the old days before automobiles were invented he was trained to follow his master's coach. Of course he made friends with the splendid horses that used to pull the old-fashioned fire engines, and he knew as well as the horses that a fire alarm meant a good run and plenty of excitement. He is a handsome dog with a strong graceful white body covered with large black polka dots.

E IS FOR ENGLISH BULL

terrier who is a nimble acrobat in white tights. With a stick in his mouth and a whirl through the air he is all set for a trapeze act that would charm a circus ringmaster. Besides being lively he is brave and a good bodyguard. He doesn't bark, but he will hang on to an attacker and never think of giving up.

F IS FOR FOX TERRIER

one of the oldest dogs in England. He is a real terrier (the word comes from the French "terre", meaning earth). He will go to the earth for his prey, digging into a hole for a fox or a badger. His coat may be short and smooth, or he may change it to one that is mostly wire-haired. He hunts balls oftener than he hunts foxes these days, and he likes to play hide-and-seek. He has kept the tireless energy that made him a good fox hunter, and is always ready to spend it in eager play. Just try teaching him tricks and see how quickly he learns!

G IS FOR GREYHOUND

who can win a sprinting contest any day. He is the fastest runner of the canine family, and for this reason he is often trained to race in an arena. He also makes a good pet and is always ready to chase a ball. He has an affectionate nature and gives a good master loyal devotion. To real dog lovers that is better than racing.

H IS FOR HUSKY ~

the dog of the Eskimo. He believes in being prepared for bad weather, so he carries his raincoat on his back. His thick tawny hair is waterproof and it keeps him warm and dry in an Arctic blizzard. He is very strong and can carry a forty pound load on his back. Often he is harnessed with other huskies to a loaded sledge and travels many miles a day over ice and snow working for his master, his harness bells jingling merrily.

I IS FOR IRISH TERRIER

full of pluck, nerve, daring and play. In Ireland where they proudly call him their National Dog he is watchdog, farm worker and guardian of the children. He is a good pal and people like him wherever he goes.

J IS FOR JAPANESE SPANIEL

a little Toy, silky and plume-tailed. He is highbred and a high stepper, but he is also lively and friendly; and, believe it or not, he is a grand little watchdog.

K IS FOR KERRY BLUE

who always wears a blue coat, sometimes light blue, sometimes dark. Because he doesn't shed hair his coat is always in fine condition. He used to herd sheep and cattle in Ireland, and that is where he learned to be so smart and such a good watchdog.

L IS FOR LLEWELLYN SETTER

a bird dog or retriever who used to live in Spain. After he went to England he became one of the favorite hunting dogs of the English. He doesn't kill anything; he retrieves, or brings shot game to the hunter. He has such a kind heart that he likes to keep an eye on other pets who are not so strong as he is.

M IS FOR MANCHESTER TERRIER

who is a small grayhound, swift and graceful with beautiful lines. He is now called after the city of Manchester, England, but his earlier name was Black and Tan, or Rat Terrier. He is the ancestor of the beautiful Doberman Pinscher. He loves attention, particularly if it leads to a nice run in the country.

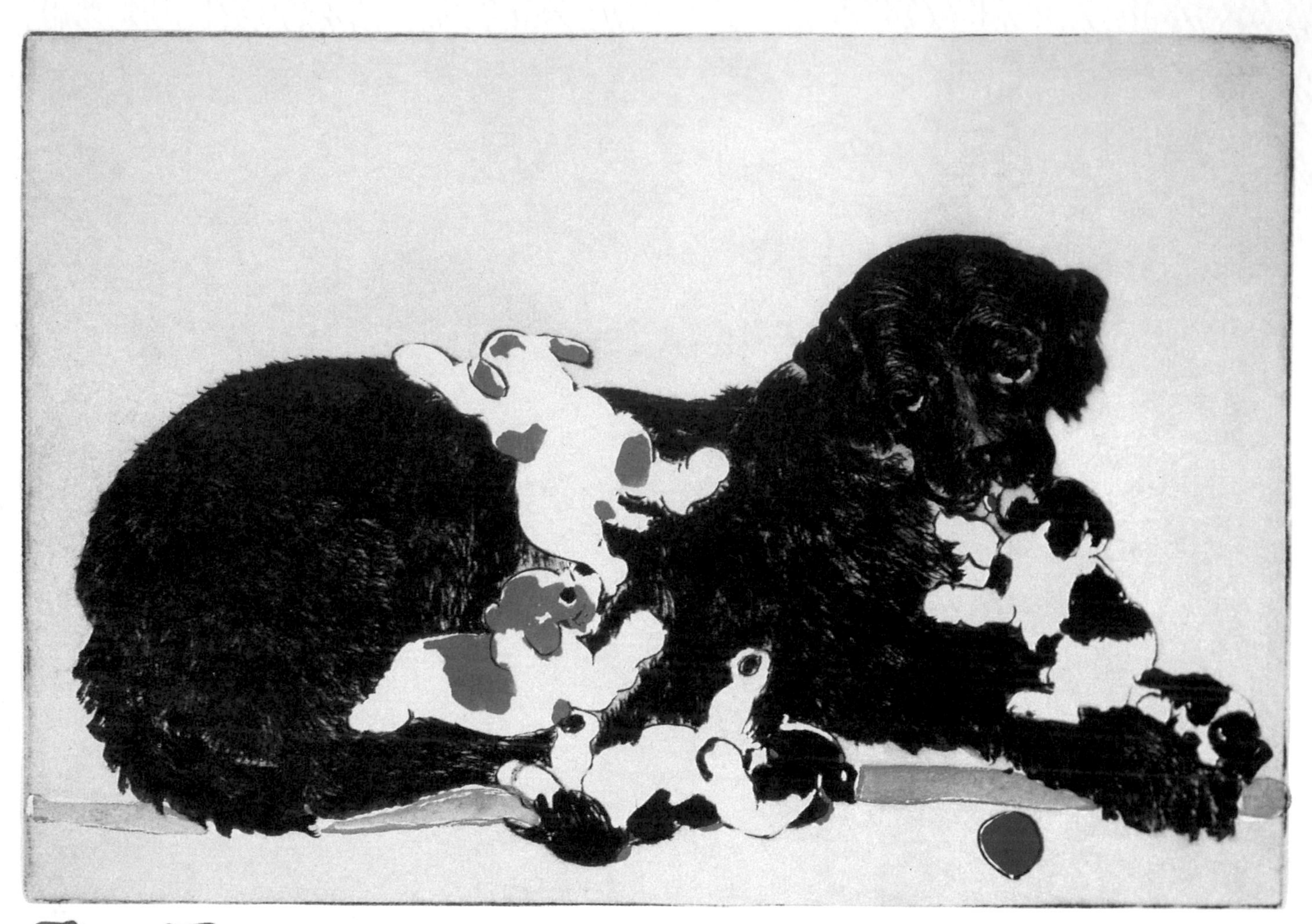

N IS FOR NEWFOUNDLAND

a furry giant of a dog, strong enough to fight a tiger and gentle enough to pull a baby's cart or carry a child on his back. He will lie in the sun and blink lazily when there is nothing else to do, but he is a splendid swimmer and has saved many people who would have drowned in a rough sea if he hadn't been quick to go to their rescue.

O IS FOR OTTERHOUND

who is fond of the water, and also a good hunter. He borrowed a coat from the Airedale and long ears and a nose from the hound. He makes such good use of that nose that the English prize him highly as a hunter. He is a brave dog and an affectionate companion.

P IS FOR POODLE

and don't ever make the mistake of thinking he isn't much good because of the strange haircut he sometimes wears. The French Poodle has quick wits behind that funny face of his. He learns tricks easily and doesn't forget them. He is strong and a good swimmer, and he also likes to play ball.

Q IS FOR QUEEN'S

Deerhound who was so highly thought of in the old days in Scotland that the nobles used to go to war and fight for him. He is so tall, stately and shaggy that he has often had his portrait painted and poets have written about him.

R IS FOR RETRIEVER

who is bold, fearless and very intelligent. There is a large family of Retrievers, among them the Golden or Long Haired, the Labrador and our own native Chesapeake Bay Retriever. The Curly-Coated Retriever looks like a baby lamb in his tight woolly coat and he likes the water almost as much as a fish does.

S IS FOR SEALYHAM

a white dog from Wales who is remarkably like the black Scotty from Scotland. Both of them are playful, lively, game little dogs. A certain little Sealyham named Jicky is my favorite companion on long hikes. She swims with me and sleeps on my bed at night. Babies love to watch her tail wag, and even when they pull it she is a good sport.

T IS FOR TOYS ~

who are so tiny that you can carry most of them in your pocket. Their shrill voices warning intruders to keep their distance may sound a little ridiculous coming from such tiny bodies, but they have staunch hearts and they intend to do their full duty as watchdogs.

(Top Row: Brussels Griffon, Mexican Hairless, Chihuahua, Papillon.
Bottom Row: Pomeranian, Italian Greyhound, Pekinese.)

U IS FOR ULMER

the old name for the Great Dane, who has a muscular body and powerful jaws. Most people, as well as other animals, take one look at him and keep out of his way, so he does not often have to use his great strength. He really has a kindly nature, perhaps because his heart like the rest of him is big and warm.

V IS FOR VENDEEN HOUND

who used to be a hunter in France. He is intelligent and loyal, but he is so excitable that he is difficult to control. In recent years breeders began changing the strain to produce the more easily managed Wire-Haired Pointing Griffon. That is why the Vendeen is rarely seen today.

W IS FOR WOLFHOUND

who has hunted wolves in Russia for centuries, and is a magnificent creature, tall, graceful and beautiful. He is devoted to his master, but is strictly a one man dog, and simply can't be bothered with friendly advances to the rest of the world.

X IS FOR JUST A DOG

whose origin is unknown and whose destiny never leads him to the Kennel Club, but often leads him to a secure place in a boy's heart. The host of mongrel dogs of strange and sometimes startling variety that belong to the great Mutt family is known far and wide for intelligence and a happy-go-lucky nature. It is these qualities that win for the Mutt friendliness and goodwill for which he gives good measure of devotion and faithfulness.

Y IS FOR YANKEE TERRIER

a good old rough-house of a dog, a wrestler, a hiker, always ready for a tug-of-war, and equally ready to be some lively boy's boon companion. He is a real American, out-of-doors dog and the best kind of watchdog.

Z IS FOR ZOOLOGICAL DOG, DINGO

otherwise known as the Dingo, the wild dog of Australia, the only dog in the Zoo. Even if you go to Australia and catch a Dingo puppy and tame him, sooner or later he will respond to the call of the wild and leave you flat. Here is one dog who goes his own way and prefers the hazards of freedom to the doubtful blessing of dependence on human whims. More power to him!